Things That Affect the Human Race

A Message of Courage & Hope

Dr. Leah M. Kelley

Blue Forge Press
Port Orchard ❀ Washington

Things That Affect the Human Race
Copyright 2020
By Leah M. Kelley

First Print Edition July 2020

ISBN 978-1-59092-981-0

All rights reserved, including the right to reproduce this book or portions thereof in any form whatsoever, except in the case of short excerpts in reviews of the book.

For information about film, reprint or other subsidiary rights, contact:
blueforgegroup@gmail.com

Blue Forge Press is the print division of the entirely volunteer-run, federal 501(c)3 nonprofit company, Blue Forge Group, founded in 1989 and dedicated to bringing light to the shadows and voice to the silence.

We strive to empower storytellers across all walks of life who strive to bring humanity together. We charge our artisans nothing and offer four divisions: Blue Forge Press, Blue Forge Films, Blue Forge Gaming, and Blue Forge Records. Find out more at:
www.BlueForgeGroup.org

To receive free access to the Dr. Kelley's sermon "Things That Affect the Human Race" please write to blueforgepress@gmail.com. And thank you for supporting an independent publisher and a courageous artisan.

DEDICATION

This book is dedicated God and to my best friend "TerryMac," may he rest in heaven. My love for you is eternal; you are deeply missed.

Also, to my six children and eleven grandchildren: I love you with an intense maternal love.

Last but never least, to my family and friends: You are loved and appreciated. Thanks to everyone who prayed for me and thanks to Geraldine A. Bowers who believed in me.

FOREWORD

In my opinion the idea to write a book of this magnitude was genius. Dr. Leah M. Kelley has a heart for the world, and as that world has been shaken with devastation, she was compelled to use her talent to bring hope, through the medium of words.

I believe that as you read each page, you will feel encouraged and empowered to live on. We must stand and fight, pray vigorously for a cure, as we band together as a nation and as a planet.

I know this may feel impossible as the world is in peril. The truth verses lies, conspiracy theories verses the facts. Troubled minds, grieving hearts, and questions all lined up like dominos. In our carnal minds we cannot begin to comprehend because it is not carnally discerned but spiritual.

This is a time to grow closer to the

Creator, bond with our families, and seek more than ever the reason for our existence.

For we all have a purpose, an assignment to be accomplished in this earthly realm.

My sentiments go out to everyone who has lost a loved one due to this pandemic. I would like to encourage you to press on and not give up. We are and you are still here for a reason.

Lastly, but definitely not least, I would like to include a special thanks for all the health professionals, doctors, and care professionals that are on the front lines fighting to take care of those suffering, and have passed away to this vicious virus.

May all of us find some level of peace and comfort in the heart-felt words of a woman of God and courageous mother.

Reuben P. Green

Dr. Kelley's Son

Things That Affect the Human Race

A Message of Courage & Hope

Dr. Leah M. Kelley

AN UNFORESEEN ENTITY

Corona virus came on the scene like a whirlwind and turned the world as we know it inside out.

It has people running around like chickens with their heads cut off, trying to avoid its sting. The precautionary measures taken are understandable and needed, but fear holds people prisoner.

Over-worked medical personnel are drained from long hours on their feet, trying everything in their power to save lives. It is mentally draining, especially all the bodies they see daily pass away.

I pray the weight of such devastation be lifted off their shoulders. Although they have been trained for this, nothing could have prepared them for the vengeance of COVID-19.

This is where we take a moment to address fear and its effects.

Fear is an unpleasant emotion, everyone has fears whether they be rational or irrational. Do not fret there is hope: You can and will overcome it. You must make a conscious decision to face it head on.

You are not alone. There are others that share this emotion. It can be crippling to some and motivating to others.

Although the world is gripped with fear, we must seek to find a sense of calm within us. And stand firm in our belief and faith.

For fear paralyzes, fear restricts movement, and fear limits. Fear hinders you from going forth, fear brings torment, and fear ultimately will destroy you if you allow it. My desire is through these troubling times that you will find peace during the storm. To do this, you must take action to eliminate

fear.

Fear is *false evidence appearing real.*

Are you fearing something that is nonexistent? Recognize your fear, face it. Do not allow it to consume you.

You have what it takes; you will conquer it. Listen: I get it. The unknown can be very scary; I am not oblivious to that. I just want you to move past your fears... and live.

Refuse fear's control over you. There are things you can change and there are things you cannot.

When you confront your fear, you no longer will be intimidated by it.

When we accept the peace that the world cannot give, our fears and anxieties will fade away. Be encouraged.

Fear can open a door and let in worry. They can go hand and hand. Which is a making of a bitter emotional cocktail.

The Lord Himself goes before you and will be with you; He will never leave you nor forsake you. Do not be afraid; do not be discouraged.

Deuteronomy 31:8

Moments of silence, feelings of uncertainty. Balance and stability is all in question. The world we once knew has become a stranger.

Business are closed, malls appear to be ghost towns, and our favorite restaurants stand empty. Someone pinch me: Is this really happening?

This is going through millions of minds, right now at this very moment. The clock is ticking, sweat rolls down one's brow. Paranoia an unwanted tenant, invites in its companion worry.

Worry is allowing one's mind to dwell on

difficulty or troubles. It behooves us not to focus on the problem but rather discover a solution to the problem. Worrying does not change the situation; it only makes it worse. But we must not add injury to upset. Sleepless nights when anxieties is at its peak leaves us with absolutely no rest.

That is not healthy at all. You must have a level head to deal with the circumstances at hand. Being able to manage your emotions is crucial. The consequences can be brutal if you do not. Worry is the poison that erodes the soul.

During these stressful times, worrying seems to be inevitable. If you allow it, worrying will get you down. But a good word, an encouraging word ,makes one glad. You have what it takes to make it, stay in the fight, and finish the race.

Hebrew 9:27 says, *For it is appointed unto man once to die, then after death there is a judgement.*

We all have an appointment to keep, no doubt there. But until that time comes, pursue every ambition and accomplish your dreams. Love, and allow yourself to be loved.

Mend relationships. Forgive and be forgiven. Heal that which is hurting, open and bleeding. Take this time given as a blessing, granted you by the God of second, third, and fourth chances.

Worrying does not get you anywhere but stressed out. Worrying is like carrying around mental baggage, that is useless and profits you nothing.

Worrying can cause illness and unwanted health problems. The scare of pending infection has many of us worried senseless. Although the concern is valid, do not allow worry to consume your thoughts. Have faith. Stay logical and keep educated.

Cast your cares upon Him that careth

for you.

1 Peter 5:7

Give all your worries and cares to God, for He cares for you. Doing this helps you remain clear-headed.

- Identify the real problem.
- Can you address the problem productively?
- Laugh.

For laughter doeth good like a medicine.

Philippians 4:6-7

Doubting the outcome or doubting the process forward will only can cause a tug of war in the soul.

We've all experienced doubt in our lives. Doubting our abilities, doubting our opinions, doubting what people have told us. Etcetera, etcetera, etcetera.

Doubt is a feeling of uncertainty, or a lack of conviction; doubting causes one to question everything around them. Especially, when you allow yourself to over-think a situation.

There are so many known factors that may cause doubt. For example:

- Past experiences and mistakes.
- The way that you were raised may play a significant part.
- The fear of failure has always been a key factor.
- Fear of one's ability or lack of ability.

Whatever the causes may be, I want you to shed the mentality of doubt. Dare to believe; faith helps to remove doubt. Do not

be afraid to fail, allow yourself to stretch outside what is familiar, beyond that which is comfortable.

There is a proverb that says: *Whatsoever a man thinketh so is that man.* Change your outlook on yourself or doubt will have you stuck. When you start doubting, you have stopped trusting Him who has your life in His hands. The Creator.

Jeremiah 29:11 is a good read. It reveals his plans, and intentions towards us:

> *For I know the plans I have for you," declares the Lord, "plans to prosper you and not to harm you, plans to give you hope and a future."*

When faced with all kinds of adversity there are a thousand emotions running amuck. You must harness those emotions before you become an emotional wreck. It can, and

most likely will, lead to discouragement.

Discouragement Is a loss of confidence or enthusiasm. When one is discouraged, they no longer feel confidant, or willing to do anything. Is it safe to say that the individual simply loses hope.

During this tragic time, there are many that are discouraged. It appears their strength has been drained out of them. I notice this every time I go out to get the basic necessities for daily living.

I see it written on the faces of everyone I come across: A gross, pale, off-in-the-distance look, bland and lifeless. I just want to wrap my arms around them and let them know it will be alright.

And I want to tell them that I understand the whole world has (in some way, shape, form, and fashion) been affected by this untimely, merciless virus.

The world is in global mourning with

unclaimed bodies, families broken, separated, an unattached physically. The virus has come through and caused all kinds of havoc. From the church steps, school auditoriums, and the halls of every capitol. Death has been working overtime, tallying all those he is assigned to. Leaving behind a world left to grieve their dead.

Grief causes deep sorrow. The land is in sorrow and as you watch the news the numbers show the death toll rising. They are not televising the people who recover as much. The media (and too many of the people watching) seem to have a fixation on giving death the spotlight.

Of course I think it is necessary to inform the world of the casualties of this virus. But I think it is equally important to televise those that have overcome, recovered and made it out alive.

I have buried love ones and I know how grief can try and lead you into

depression. I want to encourage you to be strong. Kick, cry, yell, if you want. Just don't fall into a downward spiral that you may not be able to come back from.

I suggest you pray. Or find someone you can trust to talk to. Focus on the good times you had with the person you have lost. Allow yourself to grieve and do not let anyone rush your process of healing.

When you lose someone it hurts; sometimes it hurts beyond reasoning. But your loved one, friend, husband or wife, wouldn't want you to stop living just because they transcended.

Missing them is normal. I lost someone on April 3, 2020; it came as a shock and absolutely knocked the wind out of me. I never saw it coming. I walked around numb for days. I kept saying: *How can you leave me? Why did you leave me?* I even asked: *How could you?*

The comforting factor, which came in like a knight in shinning armor, was that I knew without a shadow of a doubt he loved me. I swear I could hear him say: *Suck it up, cry baby.*

And I laughed. I laughed and the good memories became my medicine. Medicine to my soul infected by grief. No one in their right mind ever wants to lose anything—especially a family member. I was scrolling through my timeline on social media. All I saw as I scrolled was RIP. Every other post was about the loss of a family member.

Loss is the state or feeling of grief, when deprived of someone or something of value. Everyone deals with loss differently. Some cannot handle it while others seem to manage over the course of time and eventually recover.

We all hope and pray that the world will recover from the damage of COVID-19. There has been so much: The economy is

suffering. Millions are out of work. And while quarantined, some have even taken their own lives. What a travesty; it has been one obstacle after another we are forced to overcome.

There is a light at the end of the tunnel. The consolation is that this too shall pass, trouble does not last forever. Psalms states: *Weeping may endure for a night and joy cometh in the morning.*

There is a morning coming, renewed by joy and an abundance of peace. The tears will be wiped away, and the sun will shine again. Trust a brighter day is coming. Embrace this.

Prayer works; I am a living witness to its power. For this is the hour that hopelessness preys on the weak, promoting its wicked agenda which is defeat. Hopelessness and despair pick at the unhealed wounds of a nation, a city, a family, a relationship.

Pain abides in the hearts of many. To the point where it has seeped from the heart into the soul. I watched as a mother who was quarantined was in so much pain, she never thought that she was ever going to see her children again in the land of the living. Mass hysteria.

I pray for healing now: Father, in the name of Jesus, touch every wounded heart, heal them in the name of Jesus. Father, please, have compassion and extend to them your loving kindness and mercy.

Restore joy where there is none and give them the assurance that you are in control. That you, Lord, have control over every detail in our lives. And that we can give you thanks knowing no matter how it looks, everything will be alright.

Joy is associated with happiness. Triumph causes joy. You will triumph over everything that is holding you back, everything that causes you pain. Joy gives

you the energy you need to carry on.

Being the catalyst to happiness, and during theses tumultuous times, we need joy. We need to remember happier times in our lives. Reminiscee about the good times with family and friends.

Trauma can still your joy and bring about depression. Eliminate that by focusing on the positive instead of on the negative chain of events happening in the world today.

The unknown is another mystery, of course. It has its own set of emotions attached to it. They unknown is feared because what is not understood is feared naturally.

As I write this, we do not know precisely where this virus came from or exactly when it emerged or if it can be cured.

The unknown has catapulted nations worldwide into a state of horror. Once you

know something and understand it, then you have an edge, an upper hand. And with that knowledge you will know how to respond to the situation. The anxieties that arose from the unknown will fall away.

I have a few suggestions that will hopefully help you overcome your fear of the unknown.

Before I share them with you, allow me to add this one point: People often resist change because the outcome cannot be anticipated. (The outcome is unknown.) Resisting change may make things worse. Change is good—especially when change is for the betterment of oneself.

Fearing or even hating the unknown is called xenophobia. Don't be xenophobic.

Here are some ways to overcome xenophobia:

- Face the unknown.

- Educate yourself so you understand it and it is no longer so unknown.
- Locate the reason for your fear. It is a valid, logical fear?
- Ask yourself: Why am I afraid?
- Embrace the idea of change.

Uncertainties. We all have them. Whether we ever want to admit it or not. There have been moments in our lives where we have entertained and maybe even embraced uncertainty.

But being uncertain can have a grave effect on your decision making. It can affect how you trust people, makes you too skeptical, and it also has a hint of doubt attached to it.

During these perilous and unprecedented times, you might feel justified in being doubtful and uncertain. Can

you trust even the "facts" that are taking up space in your thoughts? Some of us even feel we can't trust our own governments.

We must make a conscious decision to turn off the television and disconnect from other media sometimes. To stop feeding your mind with things that are going to cause you to question everything, throwing your mind into a whirlwind of confusion.

A pandemic is a disease prevalent over a whole country or over the whole world.

This pandemic has affected us all; it does not discriminate. Lives have been lost of all colors, creeds, and religions.

This virus has spread at rapid speeds, affecting the population in extremely high numbers. The casualties are heartbreaking. Even as the world mourns, they are desperately at their wits' end with few

straight answers and no cure.

I know some are frustrated with the stay-at-home and quarantine orders. My advice to you is simple: It is better to be safe than sorry. Honestly, this pandemic that we are presently experiencing, is going to change the world as we know it.

It has already left many of Americans without a job, physical schools are closed with some opened only online. Hospitals are strained to their limits and, on top of it all, researchers are engaged in a desperate search to find a cure.

At a time like this we all need to fall on our knees, humble ourselves, and cry out for mercy and for our country and our world to be healed. The Creator can be our light in this darkened hour.

We need His divine instruction on how to make it through these dark times. This world that has turned its back on Him,

needs Him now more than ever.

God is in absolute control, even though man attempts to take His glory and refuses to recognize Him for who He is. Everything that is and was is created by Him. 2 Chronicles 7:14, speaks volumes for itself and it works in our favor if we take heed and listen:

> *if my people, who are called by my name, will humble themselves and pray and seek my face and turn from their wicked ways, then I will hear from heaven, and I will forgive their sin and will heal their land.*

He is our problem solver; He is our solution giver. America, the nation that swears it is under God, seems to act as though they are God; He does not need any country's help.

Oh ye of little faith. Where is your

faith, those that profess to believe in Him? Faith is the substance of things hoped for, the evidence of things not seen.

Do you see your healing? Do you believe He will protect you? Just a few questions to get your mind thinking.

He has not given us the spirit of fear but of power, love, and a sound mind.

I am concerned with the state of minds of not just my fellow Americans but everyone. Mental health professionals are also stating those with mental health issues are even more fragile during this time.

There have been rising reports of suicides. We must check on each other, it is not about "our four and no more." The whole world is suffering. Check on your elderly neighbor and see if they need anything.

People are experiencing "cabin fever;" they don't know how to handle being

alone and all the other changes. The rebellion against social distancing in certain areas is sickening to be. We must comply—not only for your own protection but everyone else.

It is imperative that we use wisdom during this time. We must be rational—even at a time when it seems reason has taken a vacation, even when we don't know when it will return. Respect for each other should be at the forefront of everyday living. We wrestle enough daily already just to survive.

So many lies about this pandemic are circulating around, it is hard to sort out the truth.

Conspiracy theorist are also on the rise, while all of them swear to have the answer. It's hard to know what to believe in your quest for truth.

When your belief is challenged, reach inside of yourself and take inventory when God has come through for you in the past. You cannot afford to give up now. His promises remain the same. He will not fail you.

When trial and tribulations test your faith, you must stand firm on what you believe. Refuse to be swayed by what you see or hear. Whose report will you believe? The Word says: *I shall believe the report of the Lord.*

We must seek the face of the Almighty God in a time like this, so He can tell us what we need to do, during these dire times. We need His instructions on what to do and what not to do. If we refuse to listen, we will end up regretting our decision to turn a deaf ear.

We read in John: *My sheep know my voice and a stranger they will not hear.* Logic, common sense and education are vital.

Regret will have you blaming yourself for an outcome. Regret causes intense sorrow as a result of the choice one eventually ends up making.

Save yourself from regret, regain your focus, and correct your decision not to listen... and listen!

There is something else important I also need to mention: Bitterness.

The root of bitterness can spring up at a time like this and is associated with anger. If you're an American of any party, at one time or another, you probably became infuriated at the president and everything that is going on. You might be so filled with anger and bitterness that you cannot hear what God is saying. Perhaps He is trying to get the world's attention through this pandemic.

You may become bitter at God. Asking the question: How can a loving God

allow this? Just because this is taking place, does not mean He loves mankind any less. He hates sin but does not hate His creation.

The Bible explains all the events that the world will experience prior to the second coming of Christ. Some may find that interesting reading right now but that is not the focus of my message today.

Bitterness is dangerous. When you are bitter, you desire someone else to suffer; you lack or lose compassion.

To eliminate bitterness, you must first let go of the grudge that you are holding against God. Then address and let go of all the other bitterness, the unforgiven actions or words you may be harboring against anyone else.

When you let go, you will also forgive yourself. What we need is love: Love for self, love for God, and love for one another. Love heals a multitude of wounds, covers small

faults, and promotes healing. Love is an ability.

This pandemic has given each and everyone of us time to reflect, to search our souls and discover or rediscovery what is important. Allowing us time to get reacquainted with family and friends—even if only through a digital screen.

Parents have had to spend more time with their children. Although jokes circulated about how frustrating it was having everyone stuck at home, there is nothing like a parent's love.

There is nothing as important as love.

In closing, I cannot stress this enough:

God has the last say. Let me repeat that: *God has the last say.* Do not be dismayed. Let your sorrowful heart be comforted. He hears and He knows. And all things—all things—will work out according to His purpose and His plan.

Dr. Leah M. Kelley is an American Christian who presently lives in Arizona. She enjoys filling her time with music, writing, and acting and most recently appeared in the film *Sound & Silence*. She attended Brookline College where she received her degree in Criminal Justice.

www.ingramcontent.com/pod-product-compliance
Lightning Source LLC
Chambersburg PA
CBHW050047080526
44586CB00014B/1501